The Four Elements and the Periodic Table

Rebecca Stefoff

Cavendish
Square

New York

Published in 2014 by Cavendish Square Publishing, LLC
303 Park Avenue South, Suite 1247, New York, NY 10010

CPSIA Compliance Information: Batch #WW14CSQ

All websites were available and accurate when this book was sent to press.

Library of Congress Cataloging-in-Publication Data
Stefoff, Rebecca.
The four elements and the periodic table / by Rebecca Stefoff.
   p. cm. — (Is it science?)
Includes index.
ISBN 978-1-62712-518-5 (hardcover) ISBN 978-1-62712-519-2 (paperback) ISBN 978-1-62712-520-8 (ebook)
1. Periodic law — Tables — Juvenile literature. 2. Chemical elements — Juvenile literature. 3. Periodic law - Juvenile literature. I. Stefoff, Rebecca, 1951-. II. Title.
QD467.S74 2014
546—dc23

Editorial Director: Dean Miller
Senior Editor: Peter Mavrikis
Copy Editor: Cynthia Roby
Art Director: Jeffrey Talbot
Designer: Amy Greenan
Photo Researcher: Julie Alissi, J8 Media
Production Manager: Jennifer Ryder-Talbot
Production Editor: Andrew Coddington

Printed in the United States of America

IS IT
science?

Contents

An uncut diamond—one that has not yet been shaped into a sparkling jewel. Scientists have burned gems such as this one in their quest to understand the nature of matter.

What Makes A Diamond?

Suppose you could travel back in time to ancient Greece—say, around 400 BC. And suppose you took along a big, beautiful diamond. (Why not? Time travel is fantasy, after all.)

If you met an educated Greek, showed him that diamond, and asked, "What is this made of?" he would know that it was a precious gem. But he might answer your question this way: "This hard, clear stone, shot through with glittering sparks, is made up of earth and fire."

Scratching your head, you jump back into your time machine and fast-forward to a modern chemical laboratory in the present day. Showing your diamond to a scientist, you ask her the same question: "What is this made of?" She examines the stone, performs a few tests to make sure that it's a real diamond and not a fake, and answers, "This is a nice specimen of the element carbon."

The Greek in his toga and the scientist in her lab coat each answered your question by drawing on his or her knowledge of the physical world. The difference is that today we know a great deal more about matter, the stuff that everything in the universe is made of, than the ancient Greeks did.

People used to think that all matter was made up of four (or sometimes as many as seven) ingredients called elements—things that were elemental, meaning that they were the foundation or basis of everything. Scientists now know that the universe is indeed made up of elements, but there are many more of them than the thinkers of the ancient world imagined. Combined in a vast variety of ways, elements are the true building blocks of everything we see on Earth and in space.

Scientists have learned that each element has its own unique set of properties. These features and behaviors set it apart from all other elements. The properties of elements are not random or due to wild chance. They occur in patterns—patterns so precise that scientists have used them to predict the existence of elements that had not yet been discovered.

Since the mid-nineteenth century, scientists have listed the elements according to those patterns in a chart called the periodic table. Many versions of the periodic table exist, but all of them share key features. A periodic table places each element in its proper relation to the other elements, and it encodes important information about the elements' properties.

Along the way from the four elements of the ancient world to today's periodic table, the science of chemistry was born. It studies the substances that make up matter, looking at how they are structured and how they behave and interact. For the past few centuries, the curious minds investigating matter have used a powerful tool called the scientific method.

ONE

Using the Scientific Method

Science is the search for accurate knowledge about the world. To guide them on that search, scientists rely on the scientific method, which came into wide use in the seventeenth century.

The Scientific Method

The scientific method is a process, or series of steps. There are many versions, but the basic steps are:

> Observation
>> Research
>>> Hypothesis
>>>> Test or Experiment
>>>> Conclusion
>>>>> Share and Repeat

Observation means seeing something that raises a question. For example, the eighteenth-century French scientist Antoine-Laurent de Lavoisier, sometimes called "the father of chemistry," noticed something unusual in his Paris laboratory in the early 1770s—the very early days of the science we now know as chemistry.

Lavoisier was studying combustion, which is burning. He was interested in the chemical **reactions** that took place when he burned various materials. He tested sulfur, phosphorus, and diamond. (Yes, diamonds can burn—at very high temperatures. They are a form of carbon, which is also the material of coal. Experimenters in the seventeenth and eighteenth centuries caused diamonds to combust by using powerful magnifying glasses to focus intense heat on them.)

In his experiments, Lavoisier burned carefully measured amounts of the three substances. He captured the gases given off during combustion

Antoine-Laurent de Lavoisier (1743-1794) made a major breakthrough by using the scientific method.

and weighed them. To his surprise, once the weight of the gases was compared with the weight of the materials he had used, he found that sulfur, phosphorus, and diamond all gained weight when they were burned. What could cause this?

Research means gathering data, or information, that might answer the question. Maybe the answer is already known. If it is not known, research gives the scientist data that may lead to the answer. In Lavoisier's case, he learned that an English researcher named Joseph Priestley and a Swedish one named Carl Scheele had also found that something seemed to be added when substances were burned in the open air. Lavoisier also did experiments on rusting iron and found that the reaction that turned iron into rust also produced an increase in weight.

A *hypothesis* is the next step in the scientific method. It is an educated guess based on what the scientist has observed and researched. Lavoisier's hypothesis was that the substances that burned (or rusted) were absorbing something from the air.

Testing the hypothesis shows whether or not it is the right explanation. This part of the scientific method often involves experiments. Even when a scientist cannot actually do a particular experiment, he or she must at least be able to *think* of a way the hypothesis could be tested. A scientific hypothesis must be testable. If there is no imaginable way to test a hypothesis, it can never be proved—or disproved. That removes it from the realm of science.

To test his hypothesis, Lavoisier first repeated the experiments of Priestley and Scheele. He then carried out more experiments of his own, meticulously weighing his materials at every stage.

A *conclusion* comes from tests and experiments. In this step, the scientist looks at the results of the experiments and asks,

Joseph Priestley (left) and Carl Scheele also contributed to the discovery of oxygen.

"Do these results support my hypothesis?"

If the answer is "no," the scientist adds the results to his or her observations, then thinks of a new hypothesis. Good scientists admit their mistakes and wrong ideas, because their goal is to be accurate and truthful. A good scientist is also flexible, growing and changing as new knowledge is gained.

If the answer is "yes," the scientist usually *repeats* the experiment to make sure. To be considered scientific, the result of a test or experiment has to be able to be reproduced. Scientists share their work by publishing it in **scientific journals** so that others can test it, too.

Lavoisier's conclusion was that the substances that combusted and rusted had absorbed a new, previously unknown element from the air. In 1777 he gave that element a name: oxygen. It is now known to be one of the most important elements on Earth. Vital to life, it is found in air, water, and many other chemical **compounds**, or combinations of elements. Lavoisier, Priestley, and Scheele all contributed to its discovery.

The scientific method is a powerful way learning about the world. It gives scientists everywhere a clear set of standards to meet. It is also an excellent tool for identifying **pseudoscience**.

Pseudoscience

Pseudo- (SOO-doh) at the beginning of a word means "false" or "fake." Pseudoscience is false science. It is presented as if it were scientific, but it does not meet the standards of good science.

Many pseudoscientific claims are not testable. They may be so broad or vague that they have no meaning. "Silver is the second-purest element," is an example of a pseudoscientific claim. (People used to think of gold as the "highest" or purest **metal**, followed by silver, brass, and iron. That's why a supposedly perfect time in the past is called a Golden Age, while a less ideal era may be a Silver Age.)

A scientist examining that claim might ask, "What is your definition of 'purest'? Gold and silver both occur as pure elements—that is, not mixed with any other elements. Are you

Science or Pseudoscience?

FEATURES OF SCIENCE:

- Based on scientific method

- Uses reason and logic

- Looks for physical forces to
  explain results

- Testable

- Results can be reproduced

- Published in scientific journals, and
  for the general public, too

FEATURES OF PSEUDOSCIENCE:

- Often based on tradition or folklore

- Appeals to feelings

- Explains results in mystical or mysterious ways

- May not be testable

- Results cannot be regularly reproduced

- Published for the general public,
  sometimes does not meet standards of
  scientific journals

comparing their monetary value? The temperatures at which they melt? Some spiritual or mystical meanings that you think they possess? How can we measure and agree on it?"

Pseudoscientific claims are sometimes presented as facts, but with no evidence, or with poor evidence. If there is evidence, it may be statistics or quotes with no **sources**. Without knowing exactly where a piece of information comes from, it's impossible to check that the source is reliable and the information is accurate.

Finally, pseudoscience is often based on beliefs and feelings rather than logic and reason. A pseudoscientific idea may spring from tradition, folklore, or even religious writings. However, the fact that an idea, claim, or belief is pseudoscience does not always mean that the idea cannot possibly be true. It only means that it is not science.

The scientific method has cast light on many mysteries and answered many questions. It is the basis for all the sciences, from astronomy, the study of the heavens, to zoology, the study of animals. The scientific method was an essential tool for the scientists who, over the centuries, gained the knowledge of chemistry that led to the periodic table.

From ancient times right up to today, stargazing has led people to ask, "What is the universe made of?"

TWO

Ancient Elements and Atoms

Across the ancient world, people looked at the universe around them, from the ground at their feet to the stars overhead, and asked, "What is all this made of?" As they developed ideas about matter, cultures as far apart as Babylonia (located in what is now the nation of Iraq), India, and China answered that question in very similar ways.

The Babylonians and other ancient peoples knew quite a lot about some of the materials that we now recognize as elements: iron, copper, tin, and so on. Most cultures used or at least recognized a dozen or so elements. They also used fire to melt, blend, or bake materials to make **alloys** and other useful things. They heated iron to its melting point to shape it into tools and weapons. Later, they melted copper and tin together to make a new material called bronze, which could be fashioned into useful items such as helmets and daggers. They also made pottery by cooking the water out of certain soft mineral deposits called clays. But they wanted to know what made up those materials themselves.

Looking for the Building Blocks

Ancient people were curious about the most basic building blocks of the physical world—the smallest parts that cannot be broken down still further into separate parts. That's what ancient people meant by elements, and it is how modern scientists still use the term. To the ancients, though, everything—including iron, pottery, living plants and animals, and stars—was made of just four or five basic elements in an infinite variety of combinations.

And these elements were more than the substances that made up visible, physical matter. They also had philosophical or even religious meanings. They were the forces, powers, or underlying principles that held the world together. Ancient theories of the elements were often closely linked to beliefs about the order and structure of the universe, the stages of life, and health and sickness.

The Early Elements

A Babylonian poem called the *Enuma Elish* makes one of the oldest known references to the elements. Each of the five elements—earth, ocean, fire, sky, and wind—can appear in the form of a god or goddess. The ancient Egyptians, on the other hand, usually listed only four elements: earth, water, air, and fire.

India was the birthplace of the Hindu religion, which recognized five elements. The first element created was akasha, or aether, a powerful but subtle force that fills the entire universe and everything in it, but that cannot be perceived by human senses. *Akasha* gave rise to the other four elements: earth, water, air (sometimes called wind), and fire.

In ancient China the five basic elements were wood, earth, water, fire, and metal. The Chinese elements, though, were not thought of as material building blocks. Instead, they were steps or stages in the process of change that constantly takes place throughout the universe—an unending cycle of creation and destruction. Wood feeds fire, for example, but water kills fire.

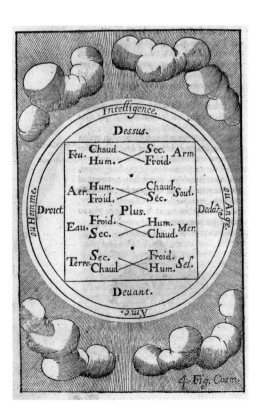

A 1657 French chart of the four elements (on left) and their properties.

The Classical Greek Elements

Ancient Greek ideas about matter formed what has been called the classical theory of the elements. This theory took shape during a period that is known as

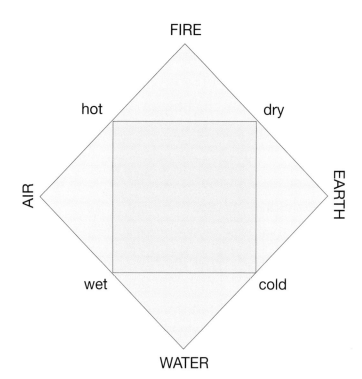

**Aristotle's classical elements
and properties.**

the Classical era in Greek history: the fifth and fourth centuries BC.

Around 450 BC a Greek philosopher and poet named Empedocles wrote that the universe is made of four elements: earth, air, fire, and water. He called these elements "roots" because they are the source and foundation of all things, just as a root is the source and foundation of a plant. Everything and everyone is made of a mixture of those elements. At the same time, the elements themselves remain pure within each mixture. They are eternal and can never be broken down. The four elements also explained the structure of the world. Earth, water, air, and fire corresponded to land, sea, sky, and sun.

During the following century, the philosopher and scientist Aristotle further developed the theory of the elements. He taught that in addition to the four elements, matter is made up of four powers or qualities: hot, dry, wet, and cold. Each element has a primary and a secondary quality. Fire's primary quality is hot, and its secondary quality is dry. Water's primary quality (surprisingly) is cold, not wet. Its secondary quality is wet. Aristotle noted that while things on Earth decay and change, the heavens never change. He decided they must be made of a superior, unchanging element, which he called aether.

This view of the universe remained in use in the Islamic world and Europe for more than a thousand years. Some later thinkers added to it with more four-part systems that matched the elements. A group called the Pythagoreans identified four stages of life: moist (springtime and youth), warm (summer and maturity), dry (autumn and old age), and cold (winter and death). The Greek physician Galen taught that the four elements and their qualities were matched by four fluids inside the body: yellow bile, black bile, phlegm, and blood. Islamic practitioners of **alchemy**—an early ancestor of chemistry—added sulfur and mercury to the original four elements.

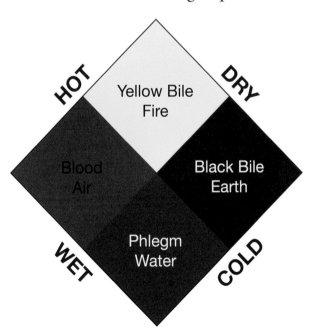

Galen's theory of the four humors, or body fluids.

Plato's Solids

Aristotle's teacher, the philosopher Plato, added a new twist to the theory of the elements. He was interested in geometric shapes—specifically, in the five shapes that are now known as platonic solids. Each of these solids has sides, or faces, that are the same size and shape as every other face on that solid. In addition, the same numbers of faces meet at every point or corner on the solid.

Plato believed that the elements were formed in these shapes. Fire was made up of four-sided tetrahedrons, with sharp, stinging points. Earth, solid and lumpy, was made of six-sided cubes (also called hexahedrons). Water flowed because it was made of smooth, twenty-sided icosahedrons. Air consisted of eight-sided octahedrons. Plato even associated twelve-sided dodecahedrons with the heavens, which Aristotle later said were made of aether, the fifth element.

Introducing the Atom

Another idea that arose in Classical Greece would prove even more long lasting and important than the theory of the four (or five) elements. That idea was atomism, from the Greek word *atomos*, meaning "uncuttable." Atomism is the notion that matter consists of two things: fundamental particles, called atoms, and empty space, called void. Matter is arrangements of atoms sticking together in various ways, with void around them and between them.

A philosopher named Leucippus and one of his pupils, Democritus, are thought to have introduced atomism to Greek philosophy in the fifth century BC. According to Democritus, all matter is made up of tiny atoms that cannot be broken or divided into smaller particles. If this sounds familiar, that's because scientists now use the term **atom** to refer to the smallest particle of any element that still has all the properties of that element.

The ancient atomists were right about matter being made of atoms, but they were wrong to think that atoms could not be broken into smaller particles. Scientists now know that atoms are made up of smaller particles. Before those discoveries could be made, however, the science of chemistry had to be born.

THREE

A New Science

Before there was chemistry, there was alchemy. Like the theory of the elements, alchemy arose in many parts of the world. Today alchemy is recognized as the ancestor or forerunner of chemistry. Alchemists, as people who practiced alchemy were called, were interested in discovering the properties of matter. They collected samples of various minerals and other materials, and then performed experiments to burn, melt, dissolve, and combine those materials. They also invented many tools and instruments that are still used in scientific laboratories today.

Alchemy had a more mystical, magical, and even religious side. Many alchemists believed that the experiments they did to "purify" materials in their laboratories would be matched by the purifying of their souls. They wanted to probe the deepest secrets of nature—not just practical secrets, such as how to produce an acid that would dissolve metal, but secrets of enormous

The modern chart of the elements is a periodic table, such as this one from the National Institute of Standards and Technology.

value. They yearned to turn low-value metals such as lead into precious ones such as gold, and to concoct a potion or powder that would cure all illnesses and allow them to live forever.

By the seventeenth or eighteenth century, the mystical side of alchemy was fading fast. The practical side of alchemy was becoming the new science of chemistry, with the scientific method as one of its most powerful tools. Using this tool and inventions such as the microscope, chemists made a series of discoveries about the nature of matter. By the middle of the nineteenth century, these discoveries had led to a whole new picture of the material world: the periodic table of the elements.

Toward Modern Chemistry

Alchemists, and later chemists, were intensely interested in materials, how to combine them, and how to change them from one state—**solid, liquid**, or **gas**—to another. Through their activities, the laws of chemistry began to be understood.

Robert Boyle of Scotland can be seen as a bridge between the dying practice of alchemy and the new science of chemistry, because he studied both. Boyle reintroduced atomism to scientific thought in his 1661 book *The Sceptical Chymist* ("skeptical chemist" in the spelling of the time). He claimed that matter was made of tiny particles called atoms that came in many shapes. The different kinds of matter were made up of differently shaped atoms combining in various ways. Boyle also deserves credit for helping to establish the scientific method. He insisted that scientists should carry out experiments to test their ideas.

Lavoisier, one of the discoverers of oxygen, made other important contributions to chemistry. In 1789 he published the first chemistry textbook. In it, he defined an element as something that could not be broken down into other substances. Lavoisier's book included a list of thirty-three of them. A few are

Finding Unknown Elements

Imagine the drama of discovering a new element! Iron, copper, sulfur, mercury, and a dozen or so other elements had been known since ancient times, but many others, never before identified, waited to be discovered by alchemists, early chemists, and adventurous travelers.

One of those new elements was the silvery-gray metal platinum. It was known to Indians in Central and South America, who often encountered it while mining silver and gold. After an Italian physician and poet named Julius Caesar Scaliger visited Central America in 1557, he wrote about this hard metal that was unknown to Europeans. Not until the eighteenth century, though, did Europeans get a detailed description and samples of platinum from Don Antonio de Ulloa, a Spanish military commander who had served in South America.

Soon all of Europe was fascinated by this gleaming new metal. It quickly became precious. Platinum remains more valuable than gold to this day, partly because it is extremely rare. Not only is platinum used to make jewelry, it is also found in industrial parts such as spark plugs and catalytic converters in cars. Platinum does not rust, tarnish, or corrode. It resists interacting with most other elements and chemical compounds.

Another discovery was made by one of Europe's last practicing alchemists, a seventeenth-century German physician named Hennig Brand. He wanted to find the philosopher's stone, a rumored substance that was believed to turn lead into gold. No one had managed to find it, but Brand thought that the secret might lie in human urine. He experimented on urine, heating and purifying it. He didn't find the philosopher's stone, but he did produce a new element that no one knew before his time: phosphorus.

Phosphorus is an unstable element that glows in the dark and bursts into flame if it is exposed to air. It caused considerable excitement among early scientists once news of Brand's discovery got around. One experimenter even reported that phosphorus set his bed on fire. Today phosphorus and chemical compounds that include it, such as phosphoric acid and calcium phosphate, are used in the manufacture of fertilizer and medical treatments. Getting hold of phosphorus no longer requires the cooking of urine, however. It is extracted from phosphate rock.

things that scientists no longer consider to be elements, such as light and heat. Most, though, are substances such as hydrogen, arsenic, tin, and other elements.

Atomic Theory

The next big step toward understanding the elements was made by an English science teacher named John Dalton. In 1803 he suggested a new atomic theory. All matter, Dalton said, was made of atoms, but each element was made of a unique kind of atom. Copper was made of copper atoms, and sulfur was made of sulfur atoms. The atoms of each element had a unique weight; this concept became known as the **atomic weight**. Atoms of different elements could combine to form compounds, such as copper sulfate.

During the 1860s, English chemist John Newlands listed the known elements by their atomic weight from lightest to heaviest, starting with hydrogen, which has an atomic weight of 1. He noticed that every element had similar physical and chemical properties to the element that was seven places away from it in the list. The first and eighth elements shared common properties, and so did the second and ninth, and so on. This kind of pattern is called periodicity, because something repeats at regular intervals, or periods. Newlands formed the hypothesis that matter has built-in periodicity.

One test of a scientific hypothesis is whether it successfully predicts new discoveries. When Newlands examined his pattern, he saw gaps or holes. He predicted that elements would be discovered to fill those holes. In 1864, for example, he predicted the existence of an element with an atomic weight of 73. Sure enough, germanium, which has an atomic weight of 73, was discovered in 1886.

Although Newlands was right, other scientists did not take his work seriously. The idea that the elements occur in periodic patterns was not widely accepted until after another chemist, Dmitri Mendeleyev, had given the world the periodic table.

four

The Map of Matter

Born in the middle of the nineteenth century, the periodic table continues to evolve today. Over the years, it has changed many times to reflect new discoveries. It has also inspired new discoveries, as scientists have labored to find—sometimes to make—the elements predicted by gaps in the table.

Today the standard form of the periodic table is a set of colored squares arranged in vertical columns and horizontal rows, like a wall built with colored blocks. Scientists have suggested other forms for the table, however, and some have even created three-dimensional versions.

Mendeleyev's Table

In the 1860s, scientists knew of between fifty and sixty elements, and new ones kept being discovered. Dmitri Mendeleyev, a Russian professor of chemistry, was writing a textbook and wanted a way to classify the elements according to their prop-

ПЕРИОДИЧЕСКАЯ СИСТЕМА ЭЛЕМЕНТОВ

ГРУППЫ ЭЛЕМЕНТОВ

ПЕРИОДЫ	РЯДЫ	I	II	III	IV	V	VI	VII	VIII	0
1	I	H 1 1,008								He 2 4,003
2	II	Li 3 6,940	Be 4 9,02	5 B 10,82	6 C 12,010	7 N 14,008	8 O 16,000	9 F 19,00		Ne 10 20,183
3	III	Na 11 22,997	Mg 12 24,32	13 Al 26,97	14 Si 28,06	15 P 30,98	16 S 32,06	17 Cl 35,457		Ar 18 39,944
4	IV	K 19 39,096	Ca 20 40,08	Sc 21 45,10	Ti 22 47,90	V 23 50,95	Cr 24 52,01	Mn 25 54,93	Fe 26 55,85 · Co 27 58,94 · Ni 28 58,69	
4	V	29 Cu 63,57	30 Zn 65,38	31 Ga 69,72	32 Ge 72,60	33 As 74,91	34 Se 78,96	35 Br 79,916		Kr 36 83,7
5	VI	Rb 37 85,48	Sr 38 87,63	Y 39 88,92	Zr 40 91,22	Nb 41 92,91	Mo 42 95,95	Ma 43 —	Ru 44 101,7 · Rh 45 102,91 · Pd 46 106,7	
5	VII	47 Ag 107,88	48 Cd 112,41	49 In 114,76	50 Sn 118,70	51 Sb 121,76	52 Te 127,61	53 J 126,92		Xe 54 131,3
6	VIII	Cs 55 132,91	Ba 56 137,36	La 57 ★ 138,92	Hf 72 178,6	Ta 73 180,88	W 74 183,92	Re 75 186,31	Os 76 190,2 · Ir 77 193,1 · Pt 78 195,23	
6	IX	79 Au 197,2	80 Hg 200,61	81 Tl 204,39	82 Pb 207,21	83 Bi 209,00	84 Po 210	85 —		Rn 86 222
7	X	— 87	Ra 88 226,05	Ac 89 227	Th 90 232,12	Pa 91 231	U 92 238,07			

★ ЛАНТАНИДЫ 58—71

Ce 58 140,13	Pr 59 140,92	Nd 60 144,27	61 —	Sm 62 150,43	Eu 63 152,0	Gd 64 156,9
Tb 65 159,2	Dy 66 162,46	Ho 67 164,94	Er 68 167,2	Tu 69 169,4	Yb 70 173,04	Cp 71 174,99

All modern periodic tables grew from the early
charts made by Russian chemistry teacher Dmitri
Mendeleyev.

erties, so that students would easily learn those properties. Like Newlands before him, Mendeleyev saw that when the elements are listed by atomic weight, certain properties repeat at regular intervals. His textbook contained a table, or chart, that listed the elements in columns by atomic weight and in rows by their properties (for example, the way they react when placed in water).

Mendeleyev published the first version of his table in 1869. A German scientist, Julius Lothar Meyer, was thinking along the same lines and created his own periodic table at the same time as Mendeleyev. However, Mendeleyev's table gained more attention, partly because he placed question marks in it to show where he expected not-yet-discovered elements to fit, and he predicted some of the properties of those unknown elements.

By the time the first of Mendeleyev's predicted elements, gallium, was discovered in 1875, scientists were already accepting his general idea for classifying the elements into a table. Mendeleyev updated his table several times to include new developments. Other chemists added to it or changed it as well. One of the most important changes grew out of new knowledge about the structure of atoms.

Inside the Atom

Atoms are the smallest units of elements, but each atom itself is made up of three particles: **neutrons** (which have no electrical charge), **protons** (which have a positive electrical charge), and

electrons (which have a negative electrical charge). The atom's **nucleus**, or center, consists of one or more neutrons and one or more protons. One or more electrons move around the nucleus in layers called electron shells.

The number of electrons in an atom is usually equal to the number of protons. With the positive and negative electrical charges balanced, the atom has no charge. But if an atom has one more electron than it has protons, or one less electron, that atom—known as an ion—will have an electrical charge, either positive or negative. Depending upon the element, an atom may have the same number of neutrons as it has protons, or more neutrons. Even within a single element, some atoms have different numbers of neutrons. These variations are called **isotopes** of the element.

An element's atomic weight is the **mass** of all the particles in one atom, but this can vary slightly because of the different masses of isotopes. The element's **atomic number** is the number of its protons. Today elements are organized in the periodic table by atomic number rather than weight, because the number is more consistent.

The Periodic Table Today

As early as the 1860s, scientists including Newlands and Mendeleyev realized that the periodic table was more than a way of organizing information about the known elements. It

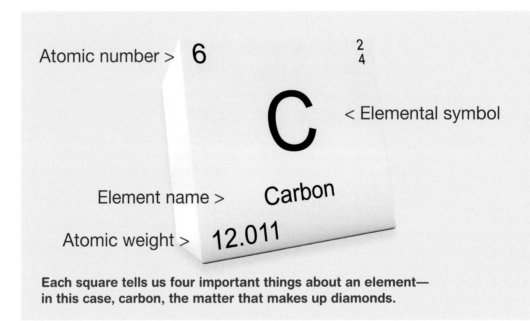

Atomic number > 6

2
4

C

< Elemental symbol

Element name > Carbon

Atomic weight > 12.011

**Each square tells us four important things about an element—
in this case, carbon, the matter that makes up diamonds.**

was a way of seeing patterns in nature. The search for what those patterns meant led eventually to a deeper understanding of how atoms are made, and how the particles inside them behave.

The periodic table had another power as well. It highlighted gaps in knowledge. For a century and a half, scientists have looked for the periodic table's "missing" elements . . . and found most of them. Most elements occur in nature. Others are synthesized, or artificially created by scientists. Some of the early **synthetic elements** were later found in nature in small amounts. Plutonium, for example, was synthesized in 1940—and used to make one of the first two atomic bombs. (The other bomb used uranium.) Plutonium is now known to occur in trace quantities in nature.

Reading the Periodic Table

The periodic table is a kind of visual code. Once you know how to read it, a single glance can tell you a lot about an element.

Start with the square that represents carbon, the sixth element in the table. It contains four pieces of key information: carbon's symbol, name, atomic number, and atomic weight. The symbol is C. The atomic number is 6, because a carbon atom has six protons in its nucleus. The atomic weight is 12.011. This is the average of the atomic weights of all known isotopes of carbon.

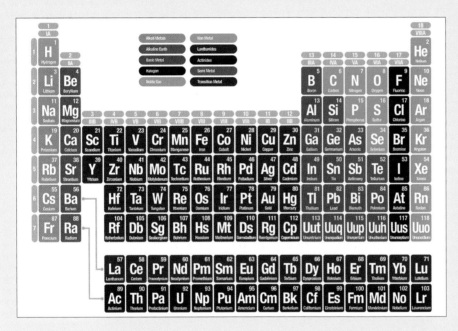

Now look at the table as a whole. Each element is in both a row and a column. A row is a period. Elements in the same period share physical properties, such as how they melt, bend, or conduct electricity. A column is a group. Elements in the same group share chemical properties, such as how they react to other elements. Notice the two gaps between elements 56 and 71, and between 88 and 104. The elements that belong in those gaps are listed in the two rows below the main chart because their electrons are arranged on electron shells in a way slightly different from the other elements.

A color-coded periodic table can tell you even more. This version uses color to identify the elements in categories such as the metals and the noble gases (the six elements that occur naturally in the form of odorless, colorless gases) and a possible seventh noble gas, the synthetic element 118, ununoctium.

Elements with atomic numbers of 99 and higher are synthetic. On Earth they can exist only in nuclear reactions or high-speed particle accelerators. These elements are so unstable that some can exist for just a fraction of a second before decaying. Teams of experts around the world work to create and study these elusive elements. In 2012, for example, Japanese researchers claimed success in producing element 113, ununtrium. They collided particles of zinc, element 30, with particles of bismuth, element 83, to produce a short-lived atom with 113 protons.

From Lavoisier's list to Mendeleyev's first table to the dazzling variations that some modern scientists and inventors have created, the periodic table has changed steadily over its lifetime. No doubt it will continue to evolve in the future. But it will remain one of the most useful tools science has ever produced for economically communicating a body of knowledge—our guide to everything that makes up the universe.

This fifteenth-century painting by Italian artist Giovanni Pietro da
Cemmo depicts four saints with the symbols of the four elements.

Glossary

alchemy	the blend of mystical philosophy and early chemistry that was practiced in the ancient and medieval worlds
alloy	material made up at least one metal, combined with at least one other metal or nonmetal, that has different properties than in the original materials; bronze is an alloy of copper and tin
atom	the smallest unit of an element that still has the unique properties of that element; atoms contain electrons revolving around a nucleus made of neutrons and protons
atomic number	the number of protons in the nucleus of an atom; each element has a different atomic number
atomic weight	the mass of one atom of an element, based on the average masses of all the isotopes of that element that are found in nature
chemistry	science of matter and its structures, properties, and reactions

compound   substance created when at least two elements are joined by chemical bonds; water is a compound of oxygen and hydrogen

electron   small particle that orbits the nucleus of an atom; has a negative electrical charge

element   basic building block of matter that has unique properties; cannot be divided into different kinds of matter

gas   a type of matter with atoms that move freely; can expand to fill any amount of space; some elements occur in nature as gases

isotope   form of an element; isotopes of the same element have different numbers of neutrons

liquid   type of matter with elements that cannot move as freely as in a gas; liquid can change shape but cannot expand in size

mass   a property of matter that has to do with the gravitational force it has on other matter and also with how much or how little it resists forces that change its speed; mass is measurement, like weight, but weight changes if gravity changes, while mass never changes

matter   physical substance or material

metal   a solid material that conducts electricity

neutron   particle in the nucleus of an atom; unlike electrons and protons, neutrons have no electrical charge

nucleus   center of an atom, made up of neutrons and protons

property   distinctive and measurable quality, feature, or behavior of an element

proton   particle in the nucleus of an atom; has a positive electrical charge

pseudoscience   false science—something that looks like science, or claims to be science, but isn't

reaction

process involving two or more elements or compounds that causes a chemical change in at least one of them

scientific journal

a magazine with articles written by scientists; before appearing in a journal, an article must be approved as scientific by a panel of experts (this is called peer review)

scientific method

a set of practical steps for answering questions about the world and adding to knowledge

solid

type of matter in which atoms cannot move

source

details about where a piece of information comes from, so that others can check to see whether the source is reliable and the information is repeated accurately

synthetic element

an element that can only be created artificially; some elements were first synthesized artificially but later found in nature in small amounts, which means that they are not true synthetic elements

Timeline

circa 600s BC	Babylonian poem *Enuma Elish* lists five basic elements: earth, sea, sky, fire, and wind
circa 450 BC	Greek philosopher Empedocles says that the four "roots" of matter are air, fire, earth, and water
400s BC	Greek philosophers Leucippus and Democritus claim that all matter is made of basic particles they call atoms
1649	German alchemist Hennig Brand discovers a new elemcnt, phosphorus
1661	Robert Boyle publishes a book on chemistry that claims that elements are made of atoms
1789	French chemist Antoine-Laurent de Lavoisier publishes the first textbook of modern chemistry, which includes a list of thirty-three elements, arranged into groups by their properties
1803	John Dalton of England develops atomic theory and measures atomic weights

1860s	English chemist John Newlands makes a table of elements that allows him to predict the existence of missing elements, which are later discovered
1869	Russian chemist Dmitri Mendeleyev publishes the first version of his periodic table; German chemist Julius Lothar Meyer publishes his periodic table one year later
1871	Mendeleyev publishes a new version of his table, with predictions of missing elements
1920s	American chemist Horace Deming gives the periodic table its present general shape
1936	Italian scientists artificially create technetium, which is later found in nature
1940s	American chemist Glenn Seaborg adds the actinide series of elements to the periodic table
1952	The first synthetic element, einsteinium, is created
2012	Japanese scientists report the creation of the synthetic element ununtrium

Find Out More

Books

Abbgy, Theodore S. *Elements and the Periodic Table.* Quincy, IL: Mark Twain Media, 2013.

Basher, Simon and Adrian Dingle. *The Periodic Table: Elements with Style!* New York: Kingfisher, 2007.

Carey, Stephen S. *A Beginner's Guide to Scientific Method.* Independence, KY: Wadsworth, 2011.

Cooper, Sharon Katz and Farhana Hossain. *The Periodic Table: Mapping the Elements.* Mankato, MN: Compass Point Books, 2007.

Glass, Susan. *Prove It! The Scientific Method in Action.* Oxford, UK: Raintree, 2006.

Green, Dan. *The Elements: Building Blocks of the Universe.* New York: Scholastic, 2012.

Ham, Becky. *The Periodic Table.* New York: Chelsea House, 2008.

Jackson, Tom. *Introducing the Periodic Table.* St. Catharines, ON: Crabtree, 2012.

Mullins, Matt. *The Elements*. New York: Children's Press, 2011.

Zannos, Susan. *Dmitri Mendeleyev and the Periodic Table*. Newark, DE: Mitchell Lane, 2004.

Websites

Chemicool
http://www.chemicool.com
This page features a colorful periodic table and a simple explanation of the table, and is packed with additional information. Click on any element for a page of details about that element, including when it was discovered and how it is used.

History of Chemistry
http://www.columbia.edu/itc/chemistry/chem-c2507/navbar/chemhist.html
This timeline shows the milestone discoveries in chemistry from ancient times to the present, with links to additional explanations.

How to Read the Periodic Table
http://www.amnh.org/ology/features/stufftodo_einstein/atommobile_read.php
The American Museum of Natural History's website offers this easy-to-follow guide to reading the periodic table.

The Path to the Periodic Table

http://www.chemheritage.org/discover/online-resources/chemistry-in-history/themes/the-path-to-the-periodic-table/index.aspx
Part of the Chemical Heritage Foundation's website, this page focuses on the scientists whose discoveries led to the periodic table we know today.

Visual Elements Periodic Table

http://www.rsc.org/periodic-table
England's Royal Society of Chemistry has created an interactive periodic table that lets you view the elements in the usual way—as colored squares in the table—or as symbols and artworks that represent each element's unique qualities. A slider lets you see how each element changes as you move the temperature from absolute zero to thousands of degrees. The History tab leads to information about the discoverer of each element.

Bibliography

Aldersey-Williams, Hugh. *Periodic Tales: A Cultural History of the Elements, From Arsenic to Zinc*. New York: HarperCollins, 2011.

Bardin, Jon. "Japanese scientists claim first synthesis of element 113." *Los Angeles Times*, September 26, 2012. http://articles.latimes.com/2012/sep/26/science/la-sci-sn-japanese-scientists-claim-first-synthesis-of-new-element-20120926,

Beckett, M.A. and A.W.G. Platt. *The Periodic Table at a Glance.* Oxford, UK: Blackwell, 2006.

Bell, Madison Smartt: *Lavoisier in the Year One: The Birth of a New Science in an Age of Revolution.* New York: Norton, 2006.

"Empedocles." **Internet Encyclopedia of Philosophy.** http://www.iep. utm.edu/empedocl,

Gordin, Michael D. A *Well-Ordered Thing: Dmitri Mendeleev and the Shadow of the Periodic Table.* New York: Basic Books, 2004.

Gray, Theodore. *The Elements: A Visual Exploration of Every Known Atom in the Universe.* New York: Black Dog & Leventhal, 2009.

Kean, Sam. *The Disappearing Spoon: And Other True Tales of Madness, Love, and the History of the World from the Periodic Table of the Elements.* New York: Little, Brown and Company, 2010.

Kingsley, Peter. *Ancient Philosophy, Mystery, and Magic: Empedocles and Pythagorean Tradition.* New York: Oxford University Press, 1995.

Moskowitz, Clara. "Quest Aims to Create Bigger Atoms and New Kinds of Matter." **LiveScience,** March 12, 2010. http://www.livescience. com/6220-quest-aims-create-bigger-atoms-kinds-matter.html.

Scerri, Eric R. *The Periodic Table: A Very Short Introduction.* New York: Oxford University Press, 2011.

———. *The Periodic Table: Its Story and Its Significance.* New York: Oxford University Press, 2006.

Index

About the Author

Rebecca Stefoff has written many books for young readers on a variety of subjects: science, exploration, history, literature, and biography. Her books about science include the four-volume series Animal Behavior Revealed (Cavendish Square, 2014), the five-volume series Humans: An Evolutionary History (Marshall Cavendish, 2010), and numerous books about animals, biology, inventions, and forensics, as well as a biography of Charles Darwin. Stefoff has also adapted bestselling science and history books by Howard Zinn, Jared Diamond, Ronald Takaki, and Charles C. Mann into versions for young readers. Learn more about Stefoff and her books at rebeccastefoff.com.